Impressum
Verlag: BABADADA GmbH, Nedderfeld 112 , 22529 Hamburg
Geschäftsführer / Verlagsleitung: Harald Hof
Druck: Books on Demand GmbH, In de Tarpen 42, 22848 Norderstedt

Imprint
Publisher: BABADADA GmbH, Nedderfeld 112 , 22529 Hamburg, Germany
Managing Director / Publishing direction: Harald Hof
Print: Books on Demand GmbH, In de Tarpen 42, 22848 Norderstedt

school

学校

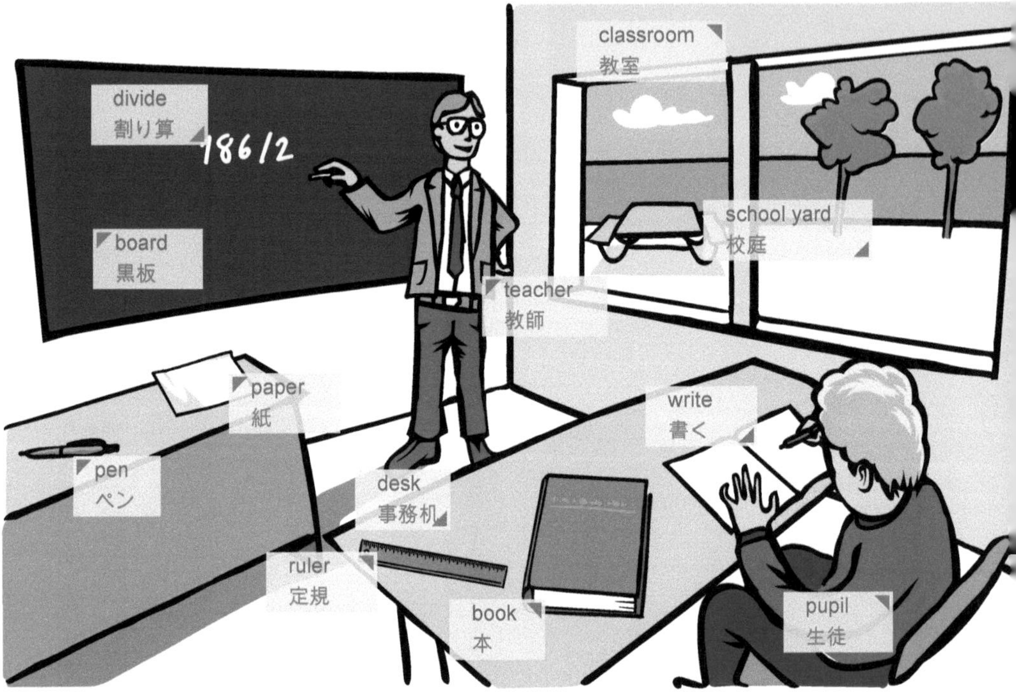

classroom
教室
divide
割り算
186/2
board
黒板
school yard
校庭
teacher
教師
paper
紙
write
書く
pen
ペン
desk
事務机
ruler
定規
book
本
pupil
生徒

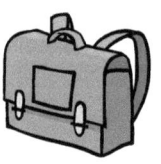

satchel

ランドセル

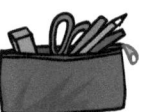

pencil case

筆入れ

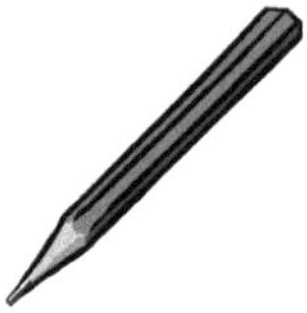

pencil

鉛筆

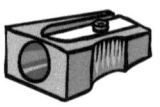

pencil sharpener

鉛筆削り

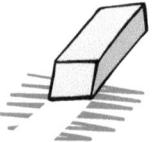

rubber

消しゴム

drawing pad

スケッチブック

drawing

スケッチ

paintbrush

絵筆

paint box

絵の具箱

scissors

はさみ

glue

接着剤

exercise book

練習帳

homework

宿題

number

数

add

足し算

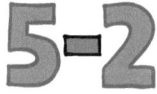

subtract

引き算

multiply

かけ算

calculate

計算する

letter

文字

alphabet

アルファベット

word

単語

text

テキスト

read

読む

chalk

チョーク

lesson

授業

register

学級日誌

examination

試験

certificate

通知表

school uniform

制服

education

教育

encyclopedia

百科事典

university

大学

microscope

顕微鏡

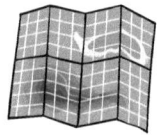

map

地図

waste-paper basket

ごみ箱

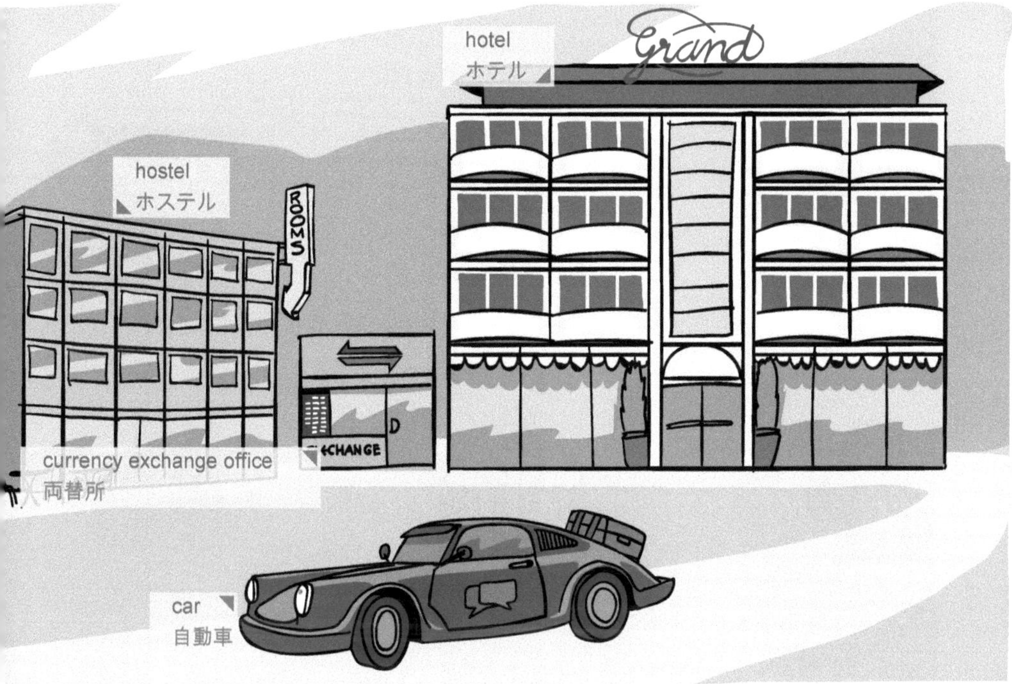

hotel
ホテル
Grand
hostel
ホステル
ROOMS
EXCHANGE
currency exchange office
両替所
car
自動車

language
言語

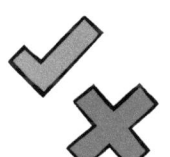

yes / no
はい / いいえ

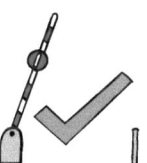

Okay
問題ない

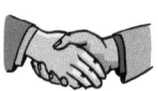

hello
ハロー

translator
翻訳者

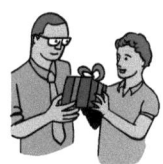

Thank you
ありがとう

how much is...?

...はいくらですか？

I don´t get it

わかりません

problem

問題

Good evening!

こんばんは！

Good morning!

おはようございます！

Good night!

おやすみなさい！

goodbye

さようなら

direction

方向

luggage

手荷物

bag

バッグ

backpack

リュックサック

guest

お客様

room

部屋

sleeping bag

寝袋

tent

テント

tourist information

旅行者情報

beach

ビーチ

credit card

クレジットカード

breakfast

朝食

lunch

昼食

dinner

夕食

Ticket

チケット

elevator

エレベーター

stamp

スタンプ

border

境界

customs

税関

embassy

大使館

visa

ビザ

passport

パスポート

transport
輸送

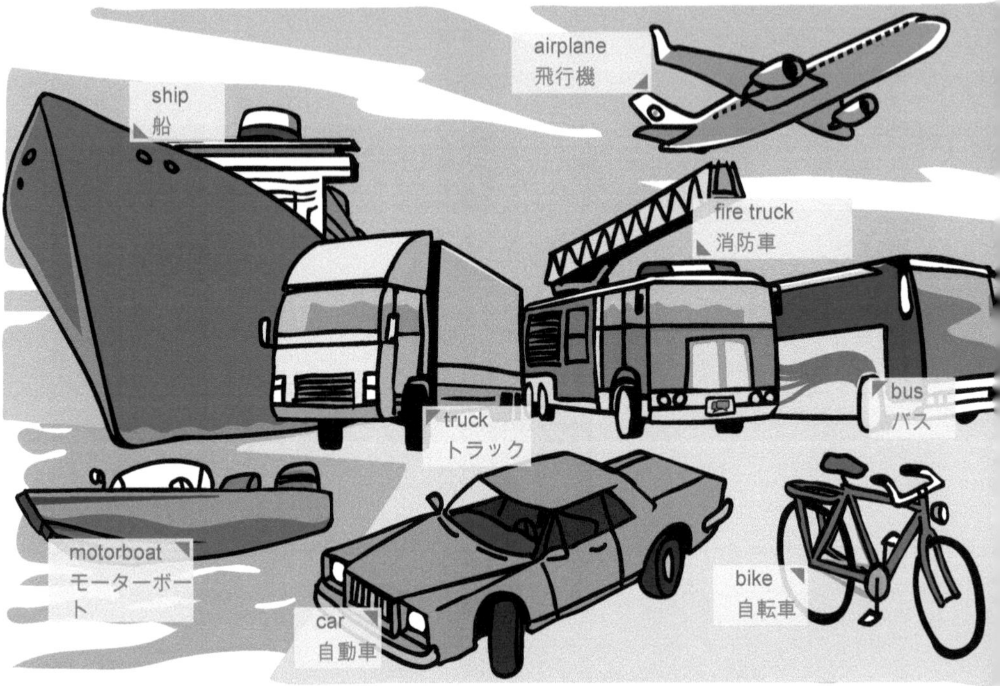
airplane
飛行機
ship
船
fire truck
消防車
bus
バス
truck
トラック
motorboat
モーターボート
bike
自転車
car
自動車

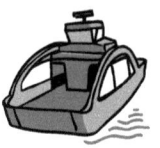

ferry

フェリー

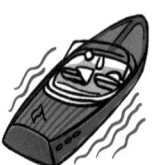

boat

ボート

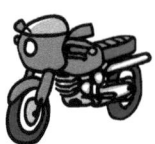

motorbike

バイク

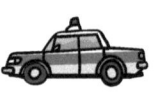

police car

パトカー

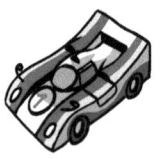

racing car

レーシングカー

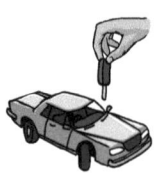

rental car

レンタカー

car sharing

カーシェアリング

tow truck

レッカー車

garbage truck

ごみ収集車

engine

モーター

fuel

燃料

˙fuel station

ガソリンスタンド

traffic sign

交通標識

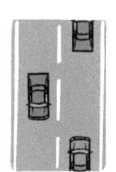

traffic

交通

traffic jam

渋滞

parking lot

駐車場

train station

駅

tracks

道

train

列車

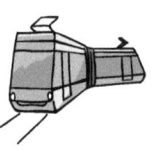

tram

路面電車

wagon

車両

helicopter

ヘリコプター

airport

空港

tower

タワー

passenger

乗客

container

コンテナ

carton

段ボール箱

cart

カート

basket

カゴ

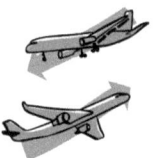

take off / land

離陸 / 着陸

city

都市

village

村

city center

都心

house

家

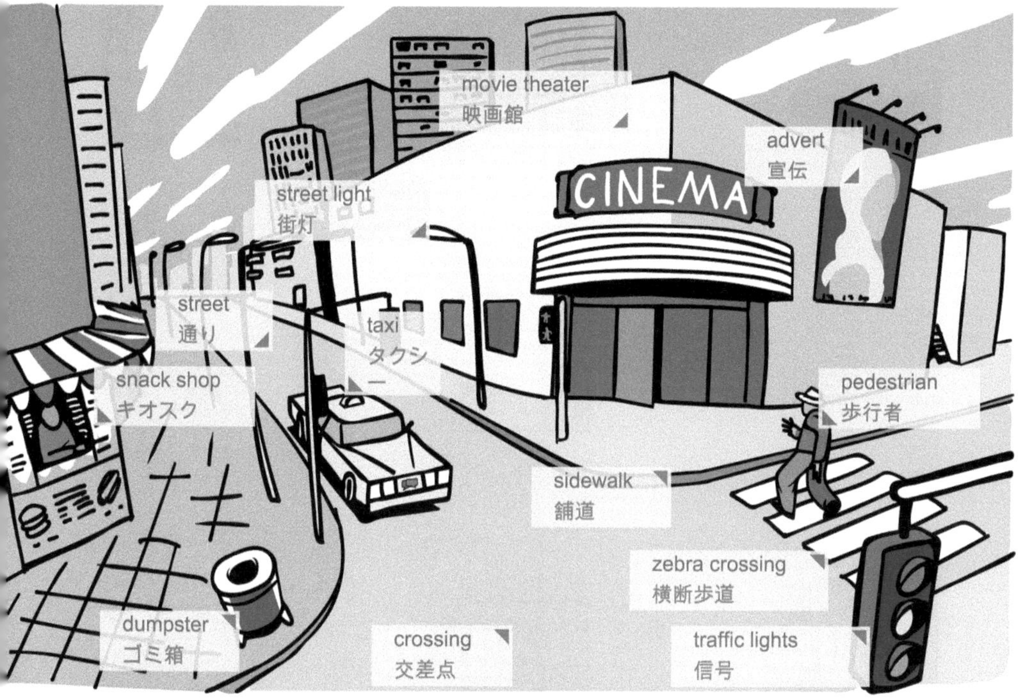
movie theater
映画館
advert
宣伝
CINEMA
street light
街灯
street
通り
taxi
タクシー
snack shop
キオスク
pedestrian
歩行者
sidewalk
舗道
zebra crossing
横断歩道
dumpster
ゴミ箱
crossing
交差点
traffic lights
信号

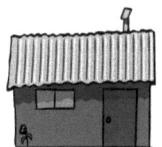

hut

小屋

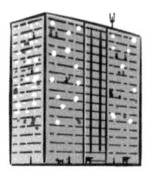

apartment

アパート

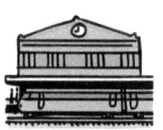

train station

駅

city hall

市役所

MUSEUM

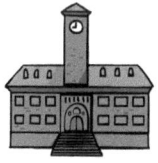

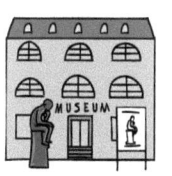

museum

美術館

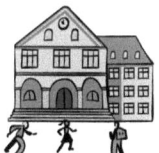

school

学校

university

大学

bank

銀行

hospital

病院

hotel

ホテル

pharmacy

薬局

office

オフィス

book shop

書店

shop

ショップ

flower shop

花屋

supermarket

スーパーマーケット

market

市場

department store

デパート

fishmonger's shop

魚屋

mall

ショッピングセンター

harbor

港

park

公園

bench

ベンチ

bridge

橋

stairs

階段

subway

地下鉄

tunnel

トンネル

bus stop

バス停

bar

バー

restaurant

レストラン

postbox

ポスト

street sign

道路標識

parking meter

パーキングメーター

zoo

動物園

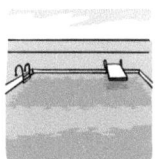

swimming pool

スイミングプール

mosque

モスク

farm

農場

pollution

汚染

cemetery

墓地

church

教会

playground

遊び場

temple

寺

landscape

風景

signpost
道標

path
道

meadow
草地

stone
石

tree
木

hiker
ハイカー

river
川

grass
草

flower
花

valley

谷

hill

山

lake

湖

forest

森

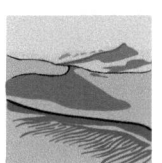

desert

砂漠

volcano

火山

castle

城

rainbow

虹

mushroom

キノコ

palm tree

ヤシの木

mosquito

蚊

fly

ハエ

ant

蟻

bee

ミツバチ

spider

クモ

beetle

カブトムシ

frog

蛙

squirrel

リス

hedgehog

ハリネズミ

hare

ウサギ

owl

フクロウ

bird

鳥

swan

白鳥

boar

雄豚

deer

鹿

moose

ヘラジカ

dam

ダム

wind turbine

風力タービン

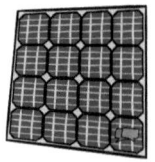

solar panel

ソーラーパネル

climate

気候

restaurant
レストラン

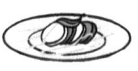

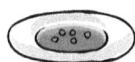

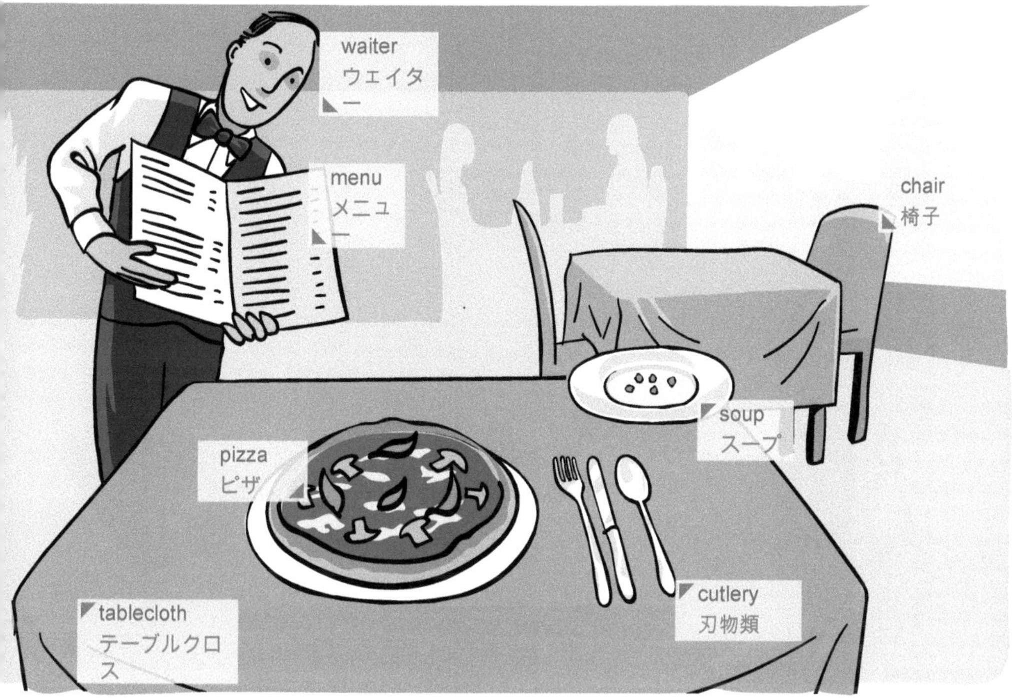

waiter
ウェイター
menu
メニュー
chair
椅子
soup
スープ
pizza
ピザ
cutlery
刃物類
tablecloth
テーブルクロス

starter
前菜

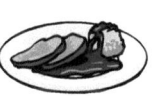

main course
メインコース

dessert
デザート

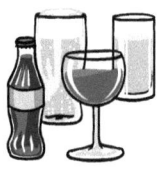

drinks
飲み物

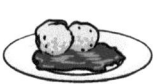

food
食べ物

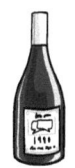

bottle
ボトル

fast food

ファストフード

street food

屋台の食べ物

teapot

ティーポット

sugar bowl

砂糖入れ

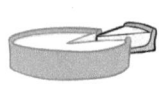

portion

一人前

espresso machine

エスプレッソマシン

high chair

幼児用食事椅子

bill

請求書

tray

トレー

knife

ナイフ

fork

フォーク

spoon

スプーン

teaspoon

ティースプーン

serviette

ナプキン

glass

グラス

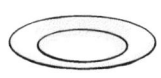

plate

皿

soup plate

スープ皿

saucer

受け皿

sauce

ソース

salt shaker

塩入れ

pepper mill

ペッパーミル

vinegar

酢

oil

油

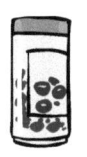

spices

スパイス

ketchup

ケチャップ

mustard

マスタード

mayonnaise

マヨネーズ

supermarket
スーパーマーケット

special offer
特価品
FOR
customer
顧客
dairy products
乳製品
fruit
果物
shopping cart
ショッピング・カート

BUTCHERS

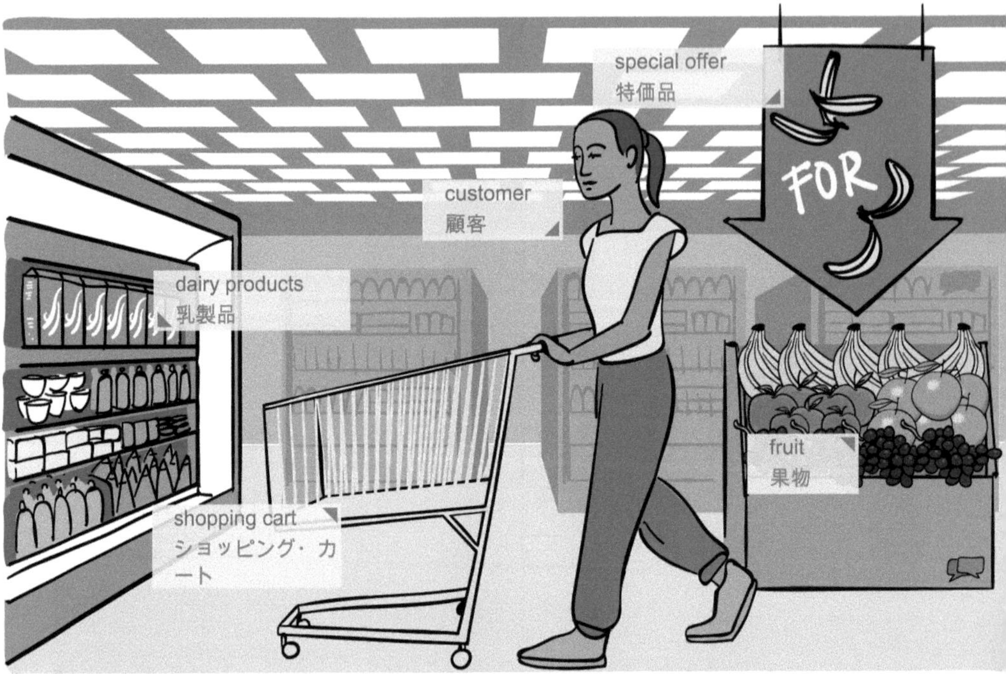

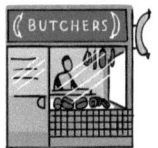

butcher's shop
肉屋

BAKERY

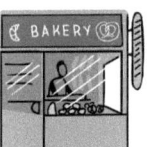

bakery
パン屋

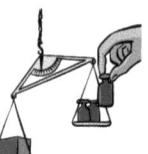

weigh
重さをはかる

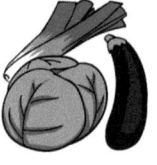

vegetables
野菜

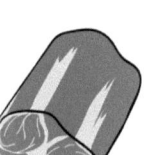

meat
肉

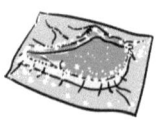

frozen food
冷凍食品

cold cuts

冷肉の薄切り

canned food

缶詰食品

detergent

洗剤

candy

菓子

household products

家庭用品

cleaning products

清掃用品

sales representative

販売員

cash register

現金箱

cashier

レジ係

shopping list

買い物リスト

opening hours

開館時刻

wallet

財布

credit card

クレジットカード

bag

バッグ

plastic bag

ポリ袋

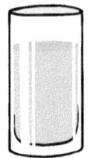

water

水

juice

ジュース

milk

牛乳

coke

コーラ

wine

ワイン

beer

ビール

alcohol

アルコール

cocoa

ココア

tea

紅茶

coffee

コーヒー

espresso

エスプレッソ

cappuccino

カプチーノ

banana

バナナ

apple

リンゴ

orange

オレンジ

melon

メロン

lemon

レモン

carrot

ニンジン

garlic

ニンニク

bamboo

竹

onion

玉ねぎ

mushroom

キノコ

nuts

ナッツ

noodles

ヌードル

spaghetti

スパゲッティ

rice

米

salad

サラダ

fries

フライドポテト

fried potatoes

フライドポテト

pizza

ピザ

hamburger

ハンバーガー

sandwich

サンドウィッチ

escalope

カツレツ

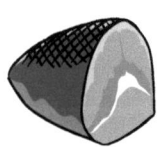

ham

ハム

salami

サラミ

sausage

ソーセージ

chicken

鶏肉

roast

焼き

fish

魚

porridge oats

麦のお粥

muesli

ムーズリ

cornflakes

コーンフレーク

flour

小麦粉

croissant

クロワッサン

bread roll

ロールパン

bread

パン

toast

トースト

cookies

ビスケット

butter

バター

curd

カッテージチーズ

cake

ケーキ

egg

卵

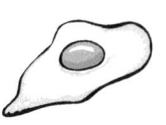

fried egg

目玉焼き

cheese

チーズ

ice cream

アイスクリーム

sugar

砂糖

honey

はちみつ

jelly

ジャム

nougat cream

ヌガークリーム

curry

カレー

farm
農場

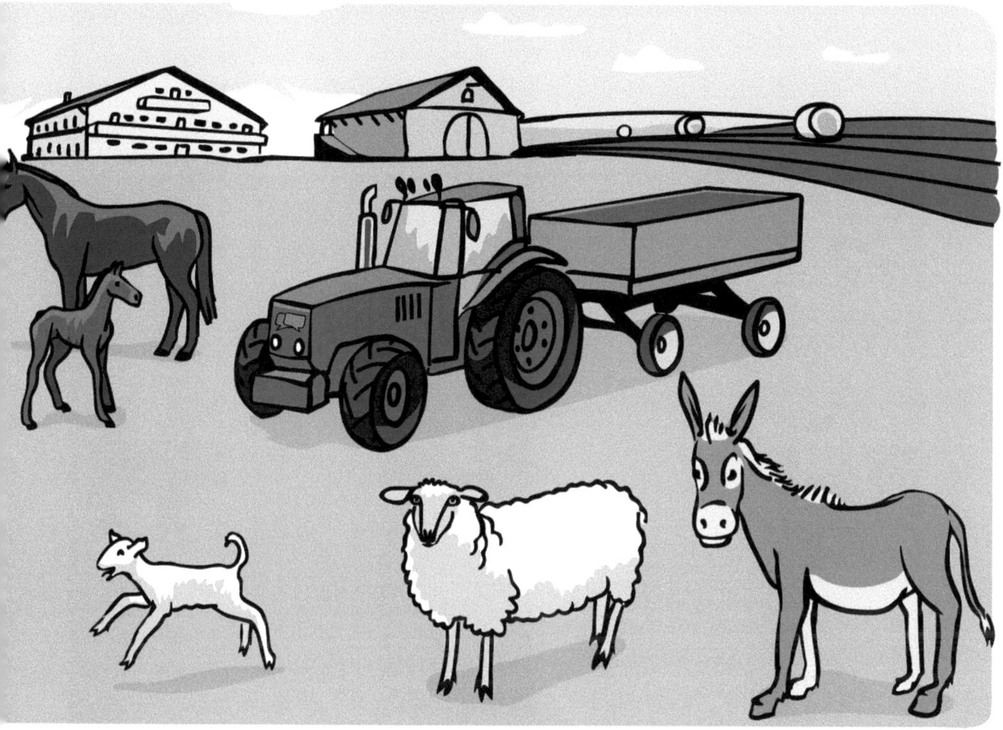

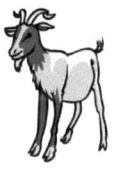

goat
ヤギ

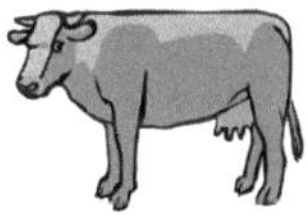

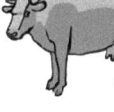

cow
雌牛

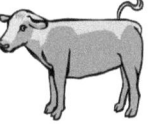

calf
子牛

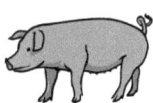

pig
豚

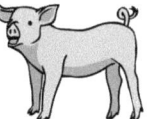

piglet
子豚

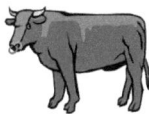

bull
雄牛

goose

ガチョウ

duck

アヒル

chick

ひよこ

hen

にわとり

cockerel

おんどり

rat

ネズミ

cat

猫

mouse

ねずみ

ox

雄牛

dog

犬

dog house

犬小屋

garden hose

散水ホース

watering can

じょうろ

scythe

大鎌

plow

すき

sickle

草刈り鎌

hoe

くわ

pitchfork

堆肥用フォーク

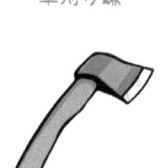

axe

斧

pushcart

手押し車

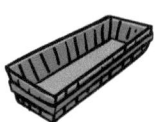

trough

かいばおけ

milk can

牛乳缶

sack

袋

fence

フェンス

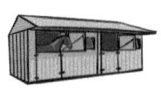

stable

畜舎

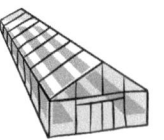

greenhouse

温室

soil

土壌

seed

種

fertilizer

肥料

combine harvester

コンバイン

harvest

収穫する

harvest

収穫

yams

ヤマイモ

wheat

小麦

soya

大豆

potato

じゃがいも

corn

トウモロコシ

rapeseed

菜種

fruit tree

果樹

manioc

キャッサバ

grain

穀物

house

家

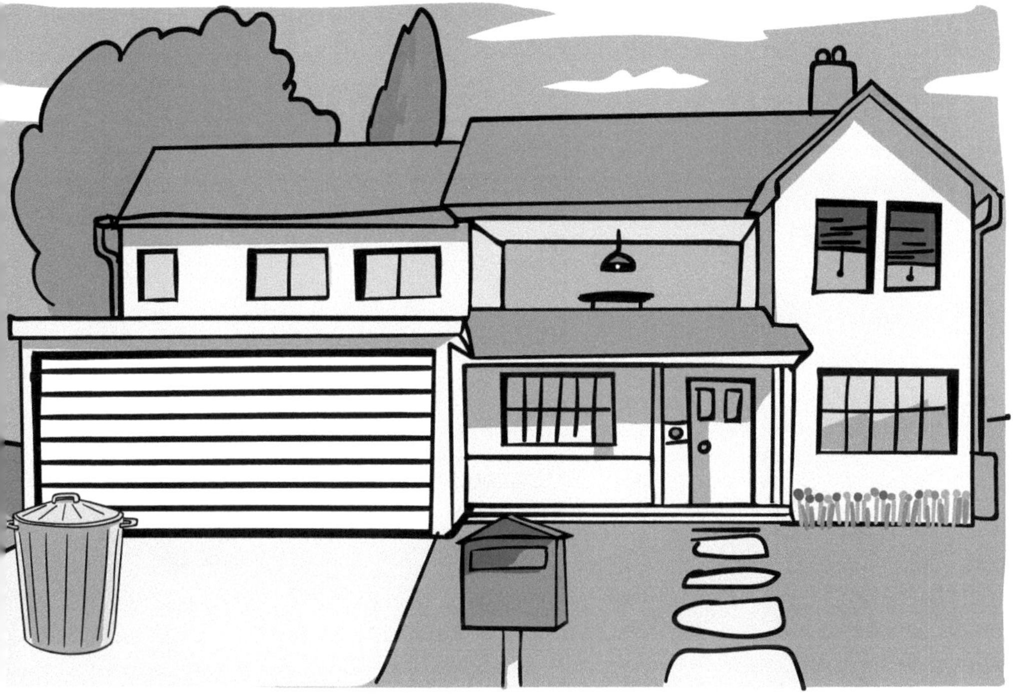

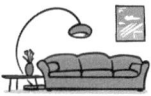

living room

リビングルーム

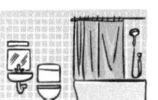

bathroom

浴室

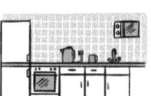

kitchen

台所

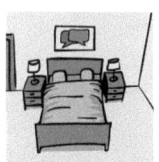

bedroom

寝室

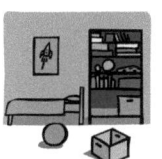

kids room

子供部屋

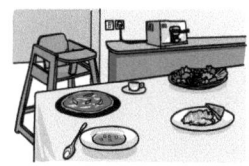

dining room

ダイニング· ルーム

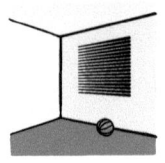

floor

床

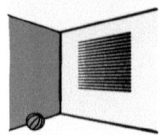

wall

壁

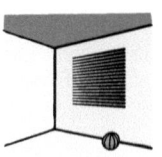

ceiling

天井

cellar

地下貯蔵庫

sauna

サウナ

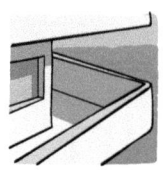

balcony

バルコニー

terrace

テラス

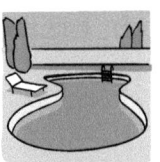

pool

プール

lawn mower

芝刈り機

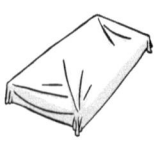

sheet

シーツ

bedspread

ベッドカバー

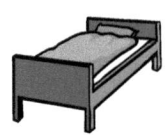

bed

ベッド

broom

ほうき

bucket

バケツ

switch

スイッチ

living room

リビングルーム

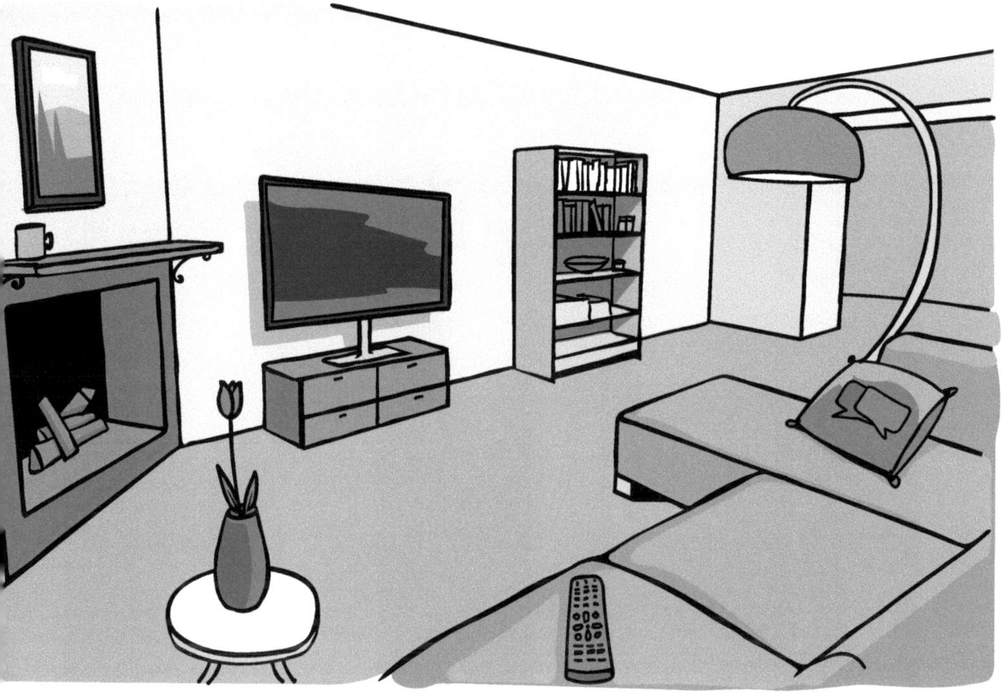

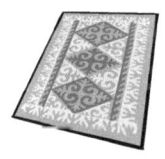

carpet

カーペット

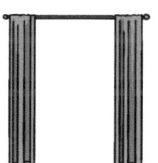

drape

カーテン

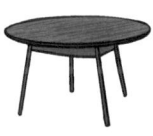

table

テーブル

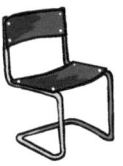

chair

椅子

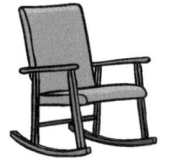

rocking chair

ロッキングチェア

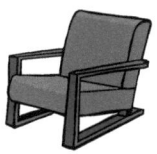

armchair

ひじ掛け椅子

book

本

blanket

毛布

decoration

飾り

firewood

たきぎ

film

映画

stereo system

ステレオ

key

鍵

newspaper

新聞

painting

絵画

poster

ポスター

radio

ラジオ

notebook

メモ帳

vacuum cleaner

掃除機

cactus

サボテン

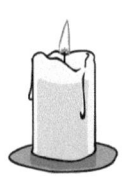

candle

ろうそく

kitchen
台所

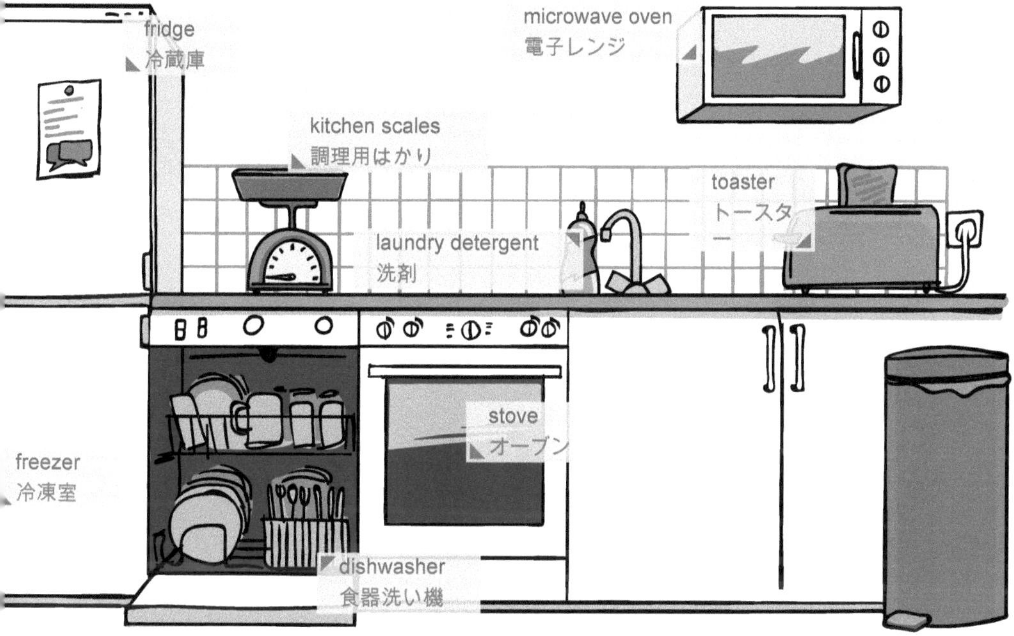

fridge
冷蔵庫
microwave oven
電子レンジ
kitchen scales
調理用はかり
toaster
トースター
laundry detergent
洗剤
stove
オーブン
freezer
冷凍室
dishwasher
食器洗い機

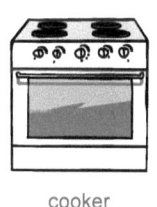

cooker
こんろ

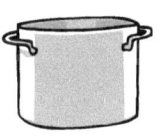

pot
鍋

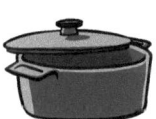

cast-iron pot
鉄鍋

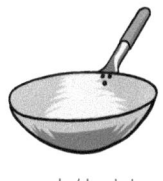

wok / kadai
中華鍋/ カダイ鍋

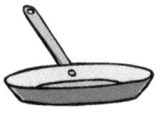

pan
フライパン

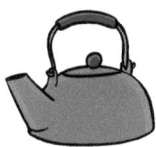

kettle
やかん

steamer

蒸し器

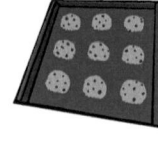

baking tray

天板

crockery

食器

mug

マグカップ

bowl

ボウル

chopsticks

箸

ladle

おたま

spatula

へら

whisk

泡立て器

strainer

こし器

sieve

ふるい

grater

すりおろし器

mortar

すり鉢

barbecue

バーベキュー

fireplace

かまど

chopping board

まな板

rolling pin

麺棒

corkscrew

栓抜き

can

缶

can opener

缶切り

oven cloth

鍋つかみ

sink

流し

brush

ブラシ

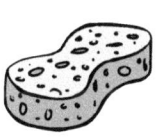

sponge

スポンジ

blender

ミキサー

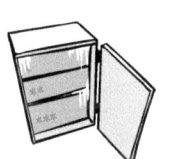

deep freezer

冷凍庫

baby bottle

哺乳瓶

tap

蛇口

bathroom

浴室

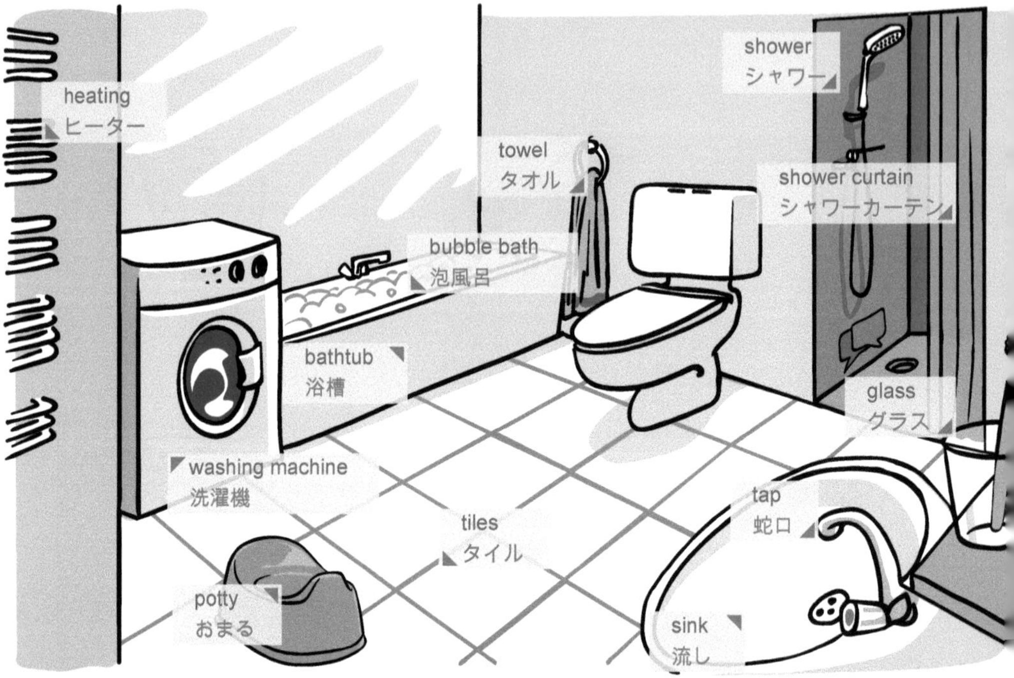
heating
ヒーター
shower
シャワー
towel
タオル
shower curtain
シャワーカーテン
bubble bath
泡風呂
bathtub
浴槽
glass
グラス
washing machine
洗濯機
tap
蛇口
tiles
タイル
potty
おまる
sink
流し

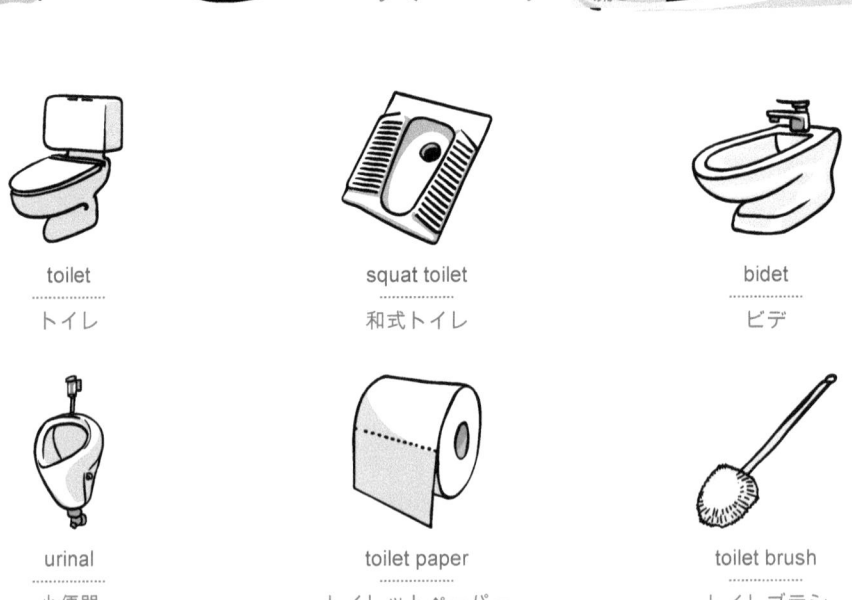

toilet

トイレ

squat toilet

和式トイレ

bidet

ビデ

urinal

小便器

toilet paper

トイレットペーパー

toilet brush

トイレブラシ

toothbrush

歯ブラシ

toothpaste

歯みがき

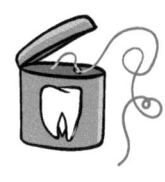

dental floss

デンタルフロス

wash

洗う

hand shower

シャワーヘッド

douche

ハンドビデ

basin

洗面台

back brush

ボディブラシ

soap

石鹸

shower gel

シャワー用ジェル

shampoo

シャンプー

flannel

浴用タオル

drain

排水口

creme

クリーム

deodorant

消臭

mirror

鏡

hand mirror

手鏡

razor

かみそり

shaving foam

シェービング・フォーム

aftershave

アフターシェーブローション

comb

櫛

brush

ブラシ

hair-dryer

ドライヤー

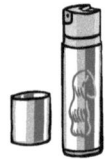

hairspray

ヘアスプレー

makeup

化粧

lipstick

口紅

nail varnish

マニキュア

cotton wool

脱脂綿

nail scissors

爪切り

perfume

香水

washbag

洗面用具入れ

stool

スツール

weighing scales

体重計

bathrobe

バスローブ

rubber gloves

ゴム手袋

tampon

タンポン

sanitary towel

生理用ナプキン

chemical toilet

ケミカルトイレ

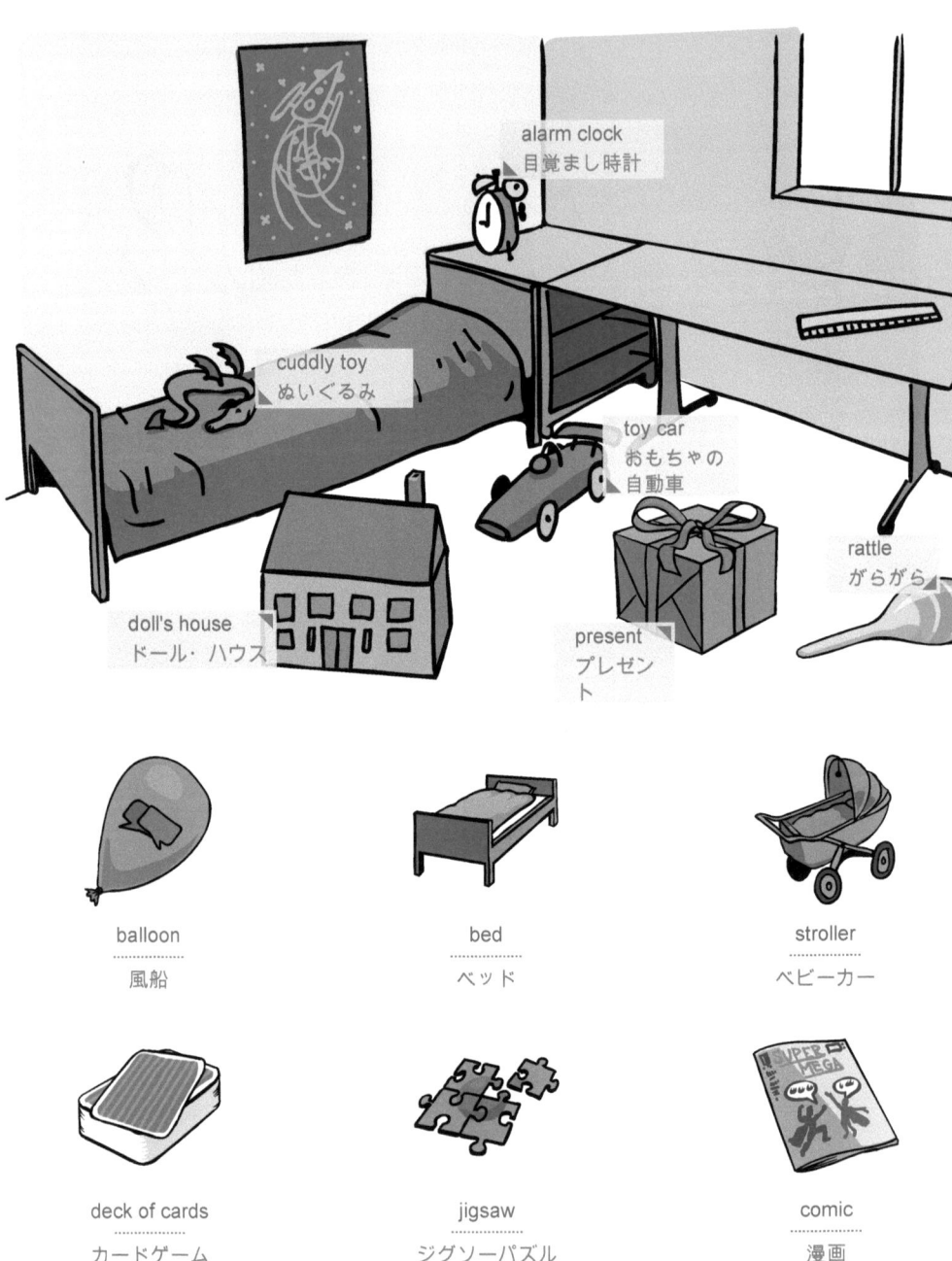

alarm clock
目覚まし時計

cuddly toy
ぬいぐるみ

toy car
おもちゃの
自動車

doll's house
ドール・ハウス

present
プレゼン
ト

rattle
がらがら

balloon	bed	stroller
風船	ベッド	ベビーカー

deck of cards	jigsaw	comic
カードゲーム	ジグソーパズル	漫画

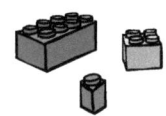

lego bricks

レゴ

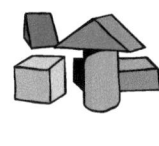

toy blocks

玩具ブロック

action figure

アクションフィギュア

romper suit

ロンパース

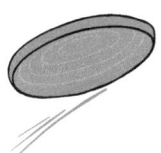

frisbee

フリスビー

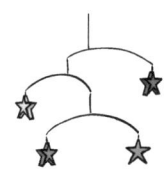

mobile

モバイル

board game

ボードゲーム

dice

さいころ

model train set

鉄道模型

pacifier

おしゃぶり

party

パーティー

picture book

絵本

ball

ボール

doll

人形

play

遊ぶ

sandpit

砂場

swing

ブランコ

toys

おもちゃ

video game console

ゲーム機

tricycle

三輪車

teddy bear

テディベア

wardrobe

衣装ダンス

clothing

衣服

socks

靴下

stockings

ストッキング

tights

タイツ

scarf
スカーフ

umbrella
雨傘

t-shirt
Tシャツ

belt
ベルト

boots
ブーツ

slippers
スリッパ

sneakers
スニーカー

sandals
サンダル

shoes
靴

rubber boots
ゴム長靴

underwear
パンツ

bra
ブラ

undershirt
ベスト

body

ボディースーツ

pants

ズボン

jeans

ジーンズ

skirt

スカート

blouse

ブラウス

shirt

シャツ

pullover

セーター

sweater

パーカー

blazer

ブレザー

jacket

ジャケット

coat

コート

raincoat

レインコート

costume

服装

dress

ドレス

wedding dress

ウェディングドレス

suit

スーツ

nightgown

ナイトガウン

pajamas

パジャマ

sari

サリー

headscarf

ヘッドスカーフ

turban

ターバン

burka

ブルカ

kaftan

カフタン

abaya

アバヤ

swimsuit

水着

trunks

トランクス

shorts

半ズボン

tracksuit

スウェットスーツ

apron

エプロン

gloves

手袋

button
ボタン

glasses
メガネ

bracelet
ブレスレット

necklace
ネックレス

ring
指輪

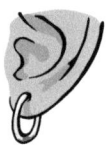

earring
イヤリング

cap
帽子

coat hanger
ハンガー

hat
帽子

tie
ネクタイ

zip
ファスナー

helmet
ヘルメット

braces
サスペンダー

school uniform
制服

uniform
ユニフォーム

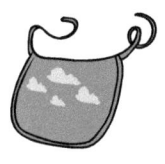

bib

よだれかけ

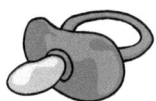

pacifier

おしゃぶり

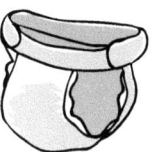

diaper

おむつ

office

オフィス

server
サーバ
filing cabinet
書類キャビネット
paper
紙
printer
プリンター
monitor
モニター
mouse
マウス
desk
事務机
folder
フォルダー
keyboard
キーボード
waste-paper basket
ごみ箱
chair
椅子
computer
コンピューター

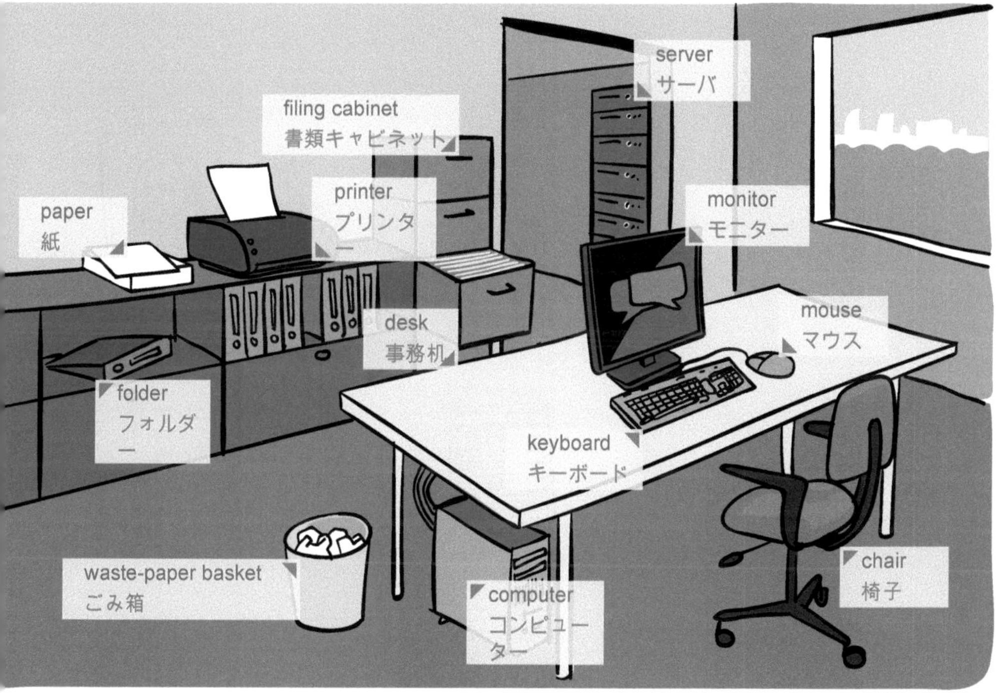

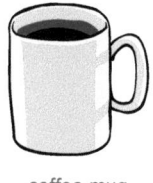

coffee mug

コーヒーマグ

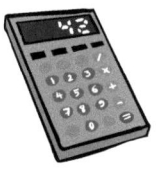

calculator

計算機

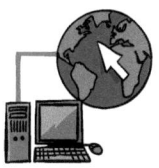

internet

インターネット

laptop

ラップトップ

letter

手紙

message

メッセージ

cell phone

携帯電話

network

ネットワーク

photocopier

コピー機

software

ソフトウェア

telephone

電話

plug socket

コンセント

fax machine

ファックス

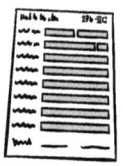

form

フォーム

document

書類

buy
買う

pay
支払う

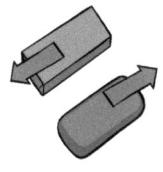

trade
取引する

money
お金

dollar
ドル

euro
ユーロ

yen
円

rouble
ルーブル

Swiss franc
スイスフラン

renminbi yuan
人民元

rupee
ルピー

cash point
キャッシュポイント

currency exchange office

両替所

gold

金

silver

銀

oil

油

energy

エネルギー

price

価格

contract

契約

tax

税金

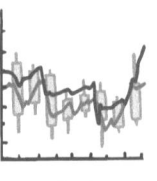

stock

株

work

働く

employee

従業員

employer

雇用主

factory

工場

shop

ショップ

occupations
職業

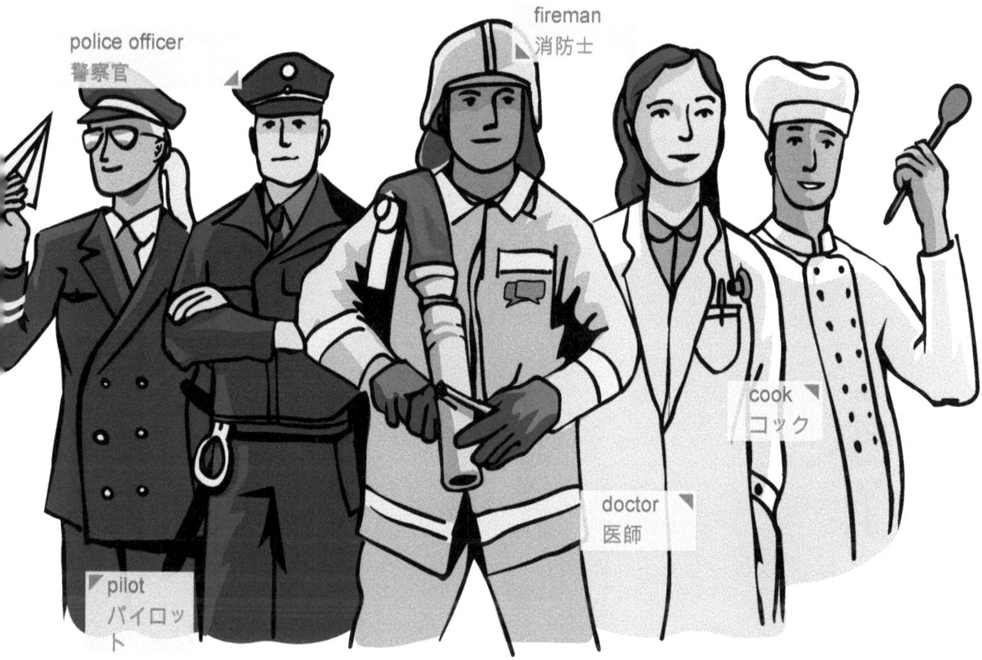
police officer
警察官
fireman
消防士
cook
コック
doctor
医師
pilot
パイロット

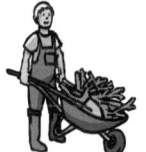

gardener

庭師

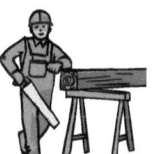

carpenter

大工

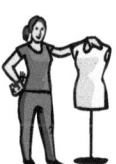

seamstress

お針子

judge

裁判官

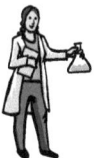

chemist

化学者

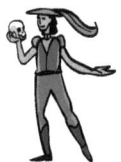

actor

俳優

bus driver

バスの運転手

taxi driver

タクシー運転手

fisherman

漁師

cleaning lady

掃除婦

roofer

屋根ふき職人

waiter

ウェイター

hunter

ハンター

painter

塗装工

baker

パン屋

electrician

電気工

builder

建設作業員

engineer

エンジニア

butcher

肉屋

plumber

配管工

postman

郵便配達人

soldier

軍人

architect

建築家

cashier

レジ係

florist

花屋

hairdresser

美容師

conductor

車掌

mechanic

機械工

captain

キャプテン

dentist

歯科医

scientist

科学者

rabbi

ラビ

imam

イスラム導師

monk

修道士

pastor

牧師

tools
道具

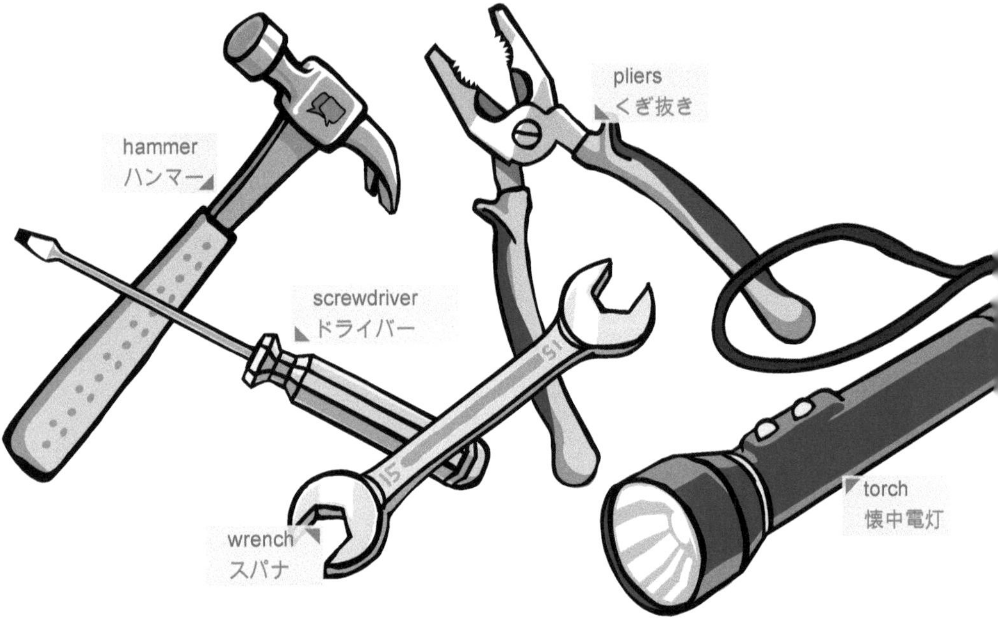

hammer
ハンマー
pliers
くぎ抜き
screwdriver
ドライバー
wrench
スパナ
torch
懐中電灯

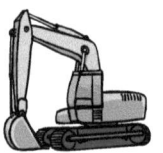

excavator

掘削機

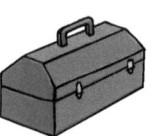

toolbox

道具箱

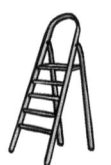

ladder

はしご

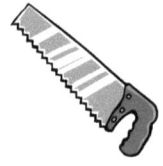

saw

のこぎり

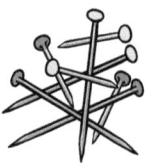

nails

釘

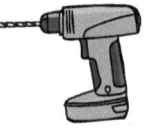

drill

ドリル

repair
修理する

shovel
シャベル

Damn!
クソ！

dustpan
ちりとり

paint can
ペンキ缶

screws
ネジ

musical instruments

楽器

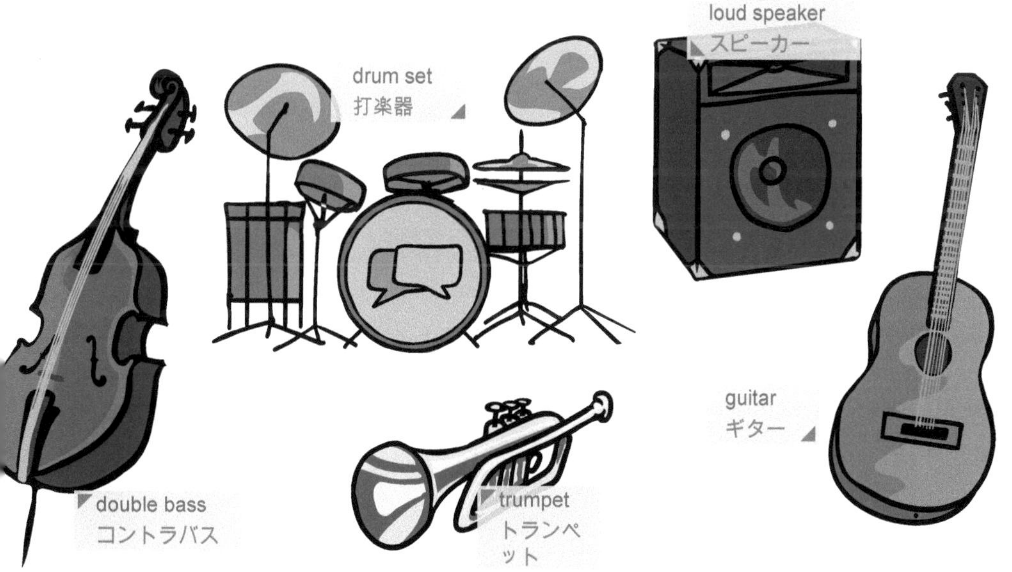

drum set
打楽器

loud speaker
スピーカー

guitar
ギター

double bass
コントラバス

trumpet
トランペット

piano

ピアノ

violin

バイオリン

bass

バス

timpani

ティンパニ

drums

ドラム

keyboard

キーボード

saxophone

サックス

flute

フルート

microphone

マイクロフォン

tiger
虎

cage
おり

zebra
シマウマ

entrance
入口

animal feed
飼料

panda
パンダ

animals
動物

elephant
象

kangaroo
カンガルー

rhino
サイ

gorilla
ゴリラ

bear
熊

camel

ラクダ

ostrich

ダチョウ

lion

ライオン

monkey

猿

flamingo

フラミンゴ

parrot

オウム

polar bear

白クマ

penguin

ペンギン

shark

サメ

peacock

クジャク

snake

蛇

crocodile

ワニ

zookeeper

飼育係

seal

アザラシ

jaguar

ジャガー

pony

ポニー

leopard

ヒョウ

hippo

カバ

giraffe

キリン

eagle

鷲

boar

雄豚

fish

魚

turtle

亀

walrus

セイウチ

fox

狐

gazelle

ガゼル

American football
アメフト

cycling
サイクリング

tennis
テニス

basketball
バスケットボール

swimming
水泳

boxing
ボクシング

ice hockey
アイスホッケー

soccer
サッカー

badminton
バドミントン

athletics
陸上競技

handball
ハンドボール

skiing
スキー

polo
ポロ

jump
跳ぶ

laugh
笑う

hug
抱きしめる

walk
歩く

sing
歌う

dream
夢見る

pray
祈る

kiss
キス

write
書く

draw
描く

show
示す

push
押す

give
与える

take
取る

have

持っている

do

する

be

ある

stand

立つ

run

走る

pull

引く

throw

投げる

fall

落ちる

lie

横たわっている

wait

待つ

carry

運ぶ

sit

座る

get dressed

着る

sleep

眠る

wake up

目が覚める

look at
見る

cry
泣く

stroke
なでる

comb
櫛ですく

talk
話す

understand
理解する

ask
質問する

listen
聞く

drink
飲む

eat
食べる

tidy up
片づける

love
愛する

cook
料理する

drive
運転する

fly
飛ぶ

sail

ヨットに乗る

calculate

計算する

read

読む

learn

学ぶ

work

働く

marry

結婚する

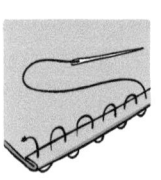

sew

縫う

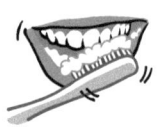

brush teeth

歯を磨く

kill

殺す

smoke

喫煙する

send

送る

grandmother
祖母

grandfather
祖父

father
父

mother
母

baby
赤ん坊

daughter
娘

son
息子

guest

お客様

aunt

おば

uncle

おじ

brother

兄弟

sister

姉妹

body

体

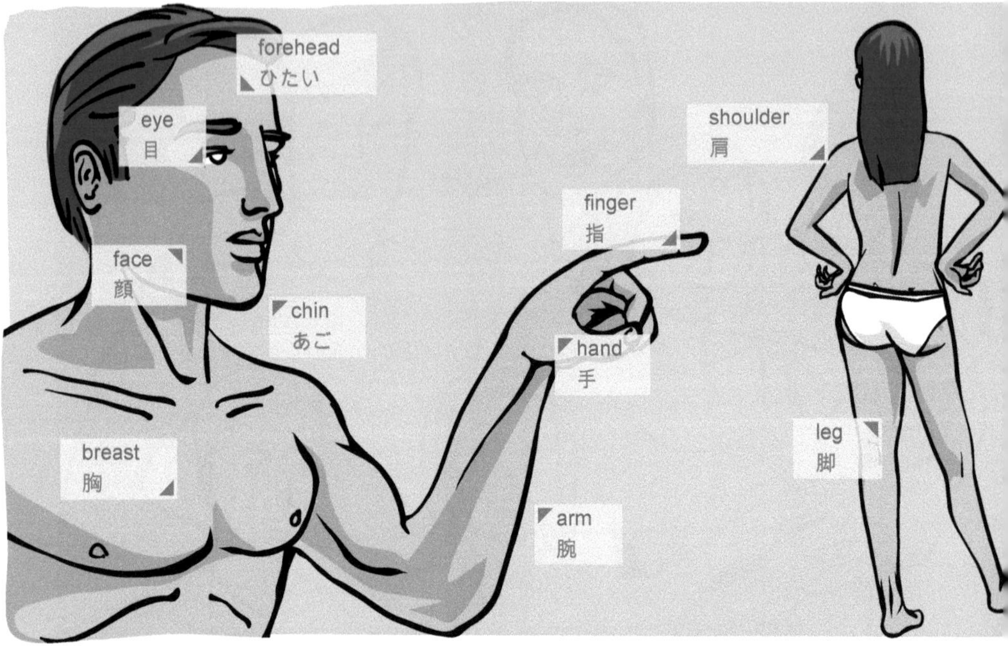

forehead
ひたい

eye
目

shoulder
肩

finger
指

face
顔

chin
あご

hand
手

breast
胸

leg
脚

arm
腕

baby

赤ん坊

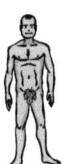

man

男性

woman

女性

girl

少女

boy

少年

head

頭

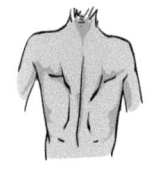

back

背中

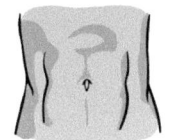

belly

腹

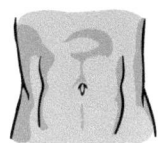

navel

へそ

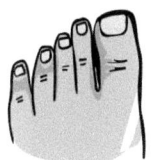

toe

足指

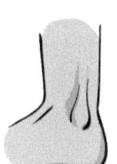

heel

かかと

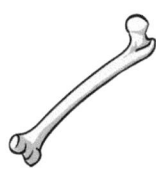

bone

骨

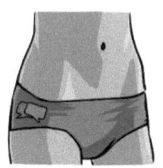

hip

腰

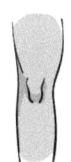

knee

ひざ

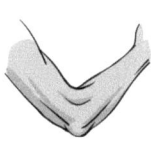

elbow

ひじ

nose

鼻

buttocks

尻

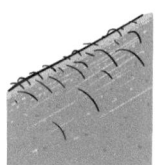

skin

皮膚

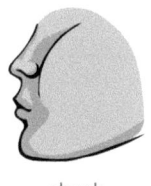

cheek

頬

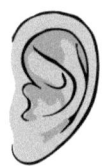

ear

耳

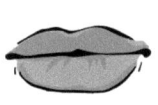

lip

唇

mouth

口

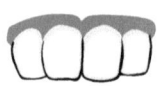

tooth

歯

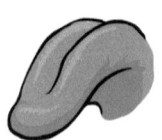

tongue

舌

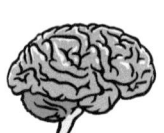

brain

脳

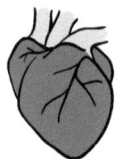

heart

心臓

muscle

筋肉

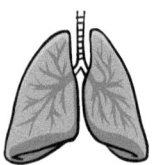

lung

肺

liver

肝臓

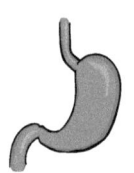

stomach

胃

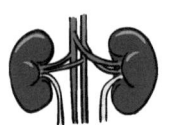

kidneys

腎臓

sex

セックス

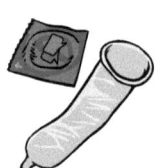

condom

コンドーム

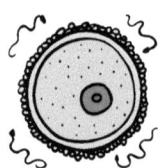

ovum

卵細胞

semen

精液

pregnancy

妊娠

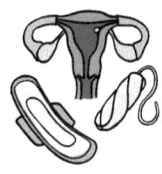

menstruation

月経

vagina

膣

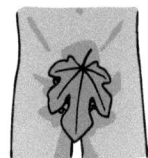

penis

ペニス

eyebrow

眉

hair

髪

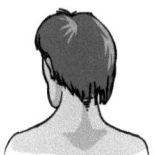

neck

首

hospital
病院

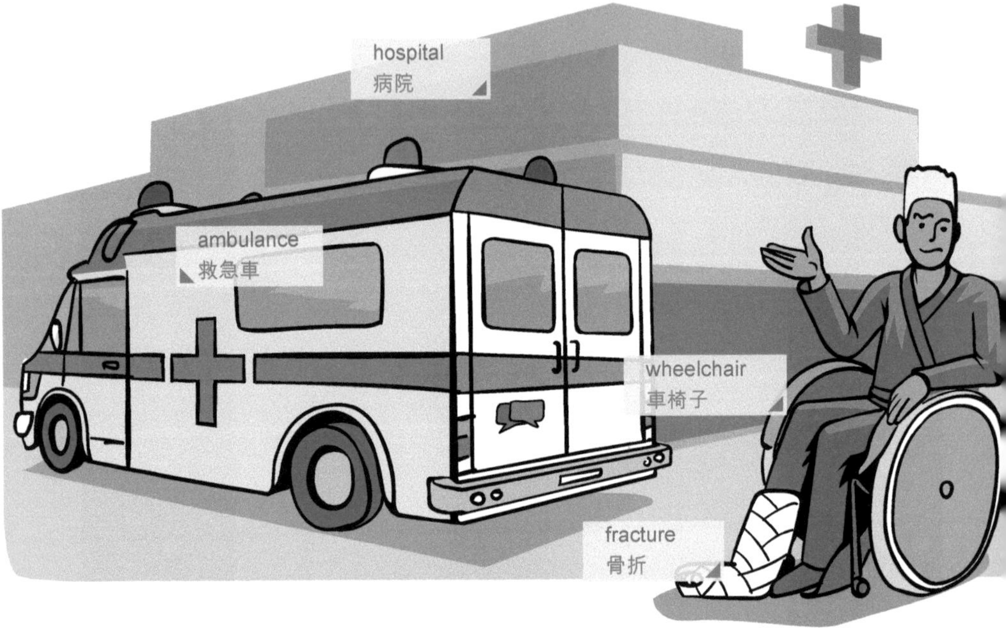

hospital
病院
ambulance
救急車
wheelchair
車椅子
fracture
骨折

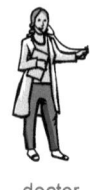

doctor
医師

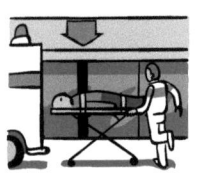

emergency room
救急治療室

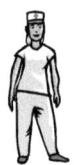

nurse
看護師

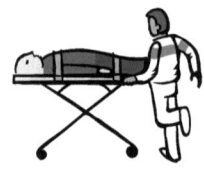

emergency
救急

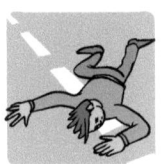

unconscious
失神

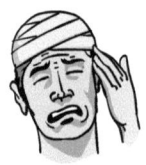

pain
痛み

injury

けが

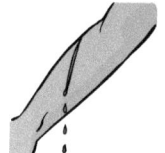

bleeding

出血

heart attack

心臓発作

stroke

脳卒中

allergy

アレルギー

cough

咳

fever

熱

flu

インフルエンザ

diarrhea

下痢

headache

頭痛

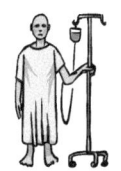

cancer

癌

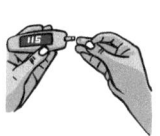

diabetes

糖尿病

surgeon

外科医

scalpel

外科用メス

operation

手術

CT

CT

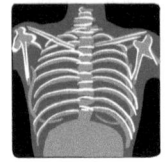

x-ray

レントゲン

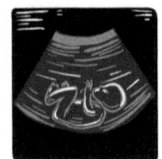

ultrasound

超音波

face mask

マスク

disease

病気

waiting room

待合室

crutch

松葉づえ

plaster

ばんそうこう

bandage

包帯

injection

注射

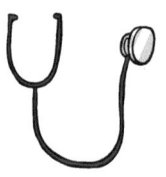

stethoscope

聴診器

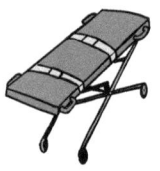

stretcher

担架

clinical thermometer

体温計

birth

出産

overweight

肥満

hospital - 病院

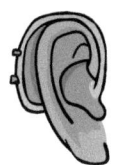

hearing aid

補聴器

disinfectant

消毒剤

infection

感染

virus

ウイルス

HIV / AIDS

HIV / エイズ

medicine

内服薬

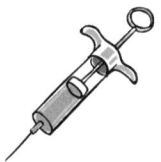

vaccination

予防接種

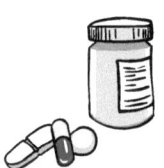

tablets

錠剤

pill

ピル

emergency call

緊急電話

blood pressure monitor

血圧計

ill / healthy

病気の / 健康な

Help!
助けて！

alarm
アラーム

assault
暴行

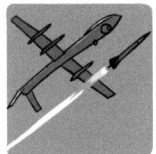

attack
攻撃

danger
危険

emergency exit
非常口

Fire!
火事だ！

fire extinguisher
消火器

accident
事故

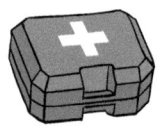

first-aid kit
救急箱

SOS
SOS

police
警察

Europe
ヨーロッパ

North America
北米

South America
南米

Africa
アフリカ

Asia
アジア

Australia
オーストラリア

Atlantic
大西洋

Pacific
太平洋

Indian Ocean
インド洋

Antarctic Ocean
南極海

Arctic Ocean
北極海

North pole
北極

South pole

南極

Antarctica

南極大陸

earth

地球

land

陸

sea

海

island

島

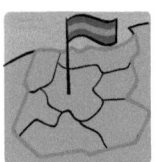

nation

国家

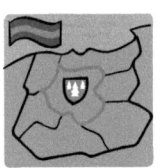

state

国家

clock face

文字盤

hour hand

短針

minute hand

長針

second hand

秒針

What time is it?

何時ですか？

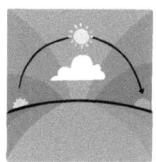

day

日

time

時間

now

現在

digital watch

デジタル時計

minute

分

hour

時間

week

週

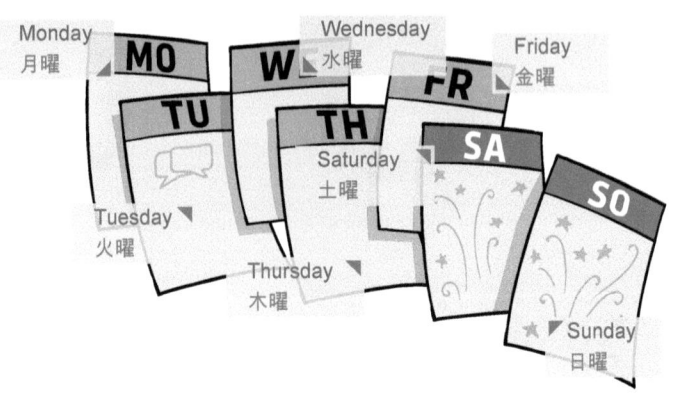

Monday 月曜 — MO
Tuesday 火曜 — TU
Wednesday 水曜 — W
Thursday 木曜 — TH
Friday 金曜 — FR
Saturday 土曜 — SA
Sunday 日曜 — SO

yesterday

昨日

today

今日

tomorrow

明日

morning

朝

noon

昼

evening

夜

workdays

営業日

weekend

週末

rain
▶ 雨

snow
雪

spring
春

wind
風

summer
夏

fall
秋

winter
冬

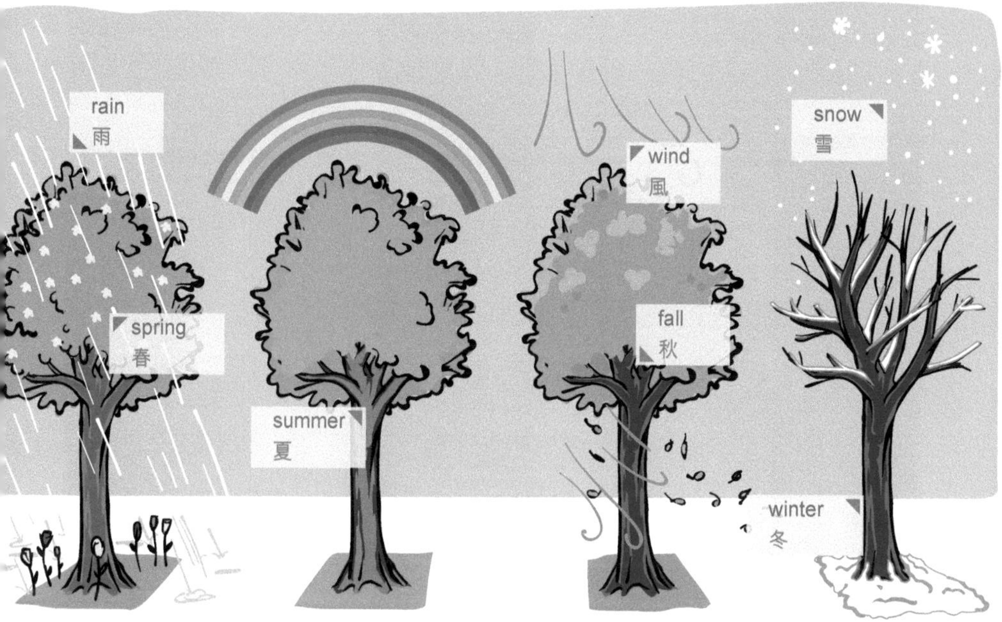

weather forecast
天気予報

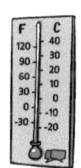

thermometer
温度計

sunshine
日差し

cloud
雲

fog
霧

humidity
湿度

lightning

雷

thunder

雷

storm

嵐

hail

ひょう

monsoon

季節風

flood

洪水

ice

氷

January

1月

February

2月

March

3月

April

4月

May

5月

June

6月

July

7月

August

8月

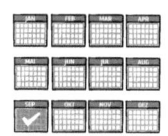

September

9月

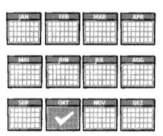

October

10月

November

11月

December

12月

shapes
形

circle

円

square

正方形

rectangle

長方形

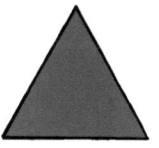

triangle

三角

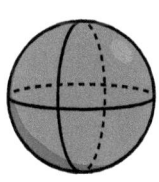

sphere

球

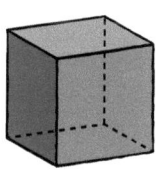

cube

立方体

white

白

yellow

黄

orange

オレンジ

pink

ピンク

red

赤

purple

紫

blue

青

green

緑

brown

茶

gray

灰色

black

黒

a lot / a little

多い　/　少ない

angry / calm

怒っている /
落ち着いている

beautiful / ugly

美しい　/　醜い

beginning / end

初め　/　終わり

big / small

大きい　/　小さい

bright / dark

明るい　/　暗い

brother / sister

兄弟　/　姉妹

clean / dirty

清潔な / 汚い

complete / incomplete

完全な　/　不完全な

day / night

日中　/　夜

dead / alive

死んだ　/　生きている

wide / narrow

幅広い　/　狭い

edible / inedible

食べられる　/
食べられない

evil / kind

悪意のある　/　親切な

excited / bored

興奮している　/
退屈している

fat / thin

太った　/　痩せた

first / last

最初に　/　最後に

friend / enemy

友人　/　敵

full / empty

いっぱいの　/　空の

hard / soft

硬い　/　柔らかい

heavy / light

重い　/　軽い

hunger / thirst

空腹　/　喉の渇き

ill / healthy

病気の　/　健康な

illegal / legal

違法な　/　合法な

intelligent / stupid

賢い　/　愚かな

left / right

左に　/　右に

near / far

近い　/　遠い

new / used

新しい / 中古の

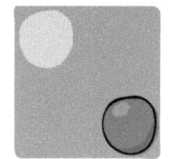

nothing / something

何もない / 何かある

old / young

老いた / 若い

on / off

オン / オフ

open / closed

開いている /
閉まっている

quiet / loud

静かな / うるさい

rich / poor

裕福な / 貧乏な

right / wrong

正しい / 間違っている

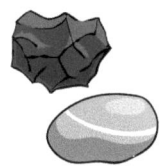

rough / smooth

粗い / なめらか

sad / happy

悲しい / 幸せな

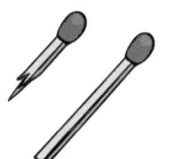

short / long

短い / 長い

slow / fast

ゆっくり / 速い

wet / dry

濡れた / 乾いた

warm / cool

温かい / 冷たい

war / peace

戦争 / 平和

数

0

zero
ゼロ

1

one
1

2

two
2

3

three
3

4

four
4

5

five
5

6

six
6

7

seven
7

8

eight
8

9

nine
9

10

ten
10

11

eleven
11

12

twelve

12

13

thirteen

13

14

fourteen

14

15

fifteen

15

16

sixteen

16

17

seventeen

17

18

eighteen

18

19

nineteen

19

20

twenty

20

100

hundred

100

1.000

thousand

1000

1.000.000

million

100万

languages

言語

English

英語

American English

アメリカ英語

Chinese Mandarin

中国標準語

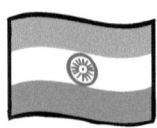

Hindi

ヒンディー語

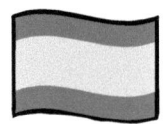

Spanish

スペイン語

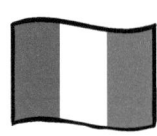

French

フランス語

Arabic

アラビア語

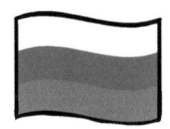

Russian

ロシア語

Portuguese

ポルトガル語

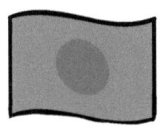

Bengali

ベンガル語

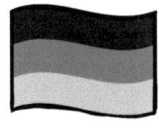

German

ドイツ語

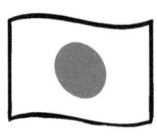

Japanese

日本語

I

私

you

あなた

he / she / it

彼 / 彼女 / それ

we

私たち

you

あなたたち

they

彼ら

who?

誰？

what?

何？

how?

どうやって？

where?

どこ？

when?

いつ？

name

名前

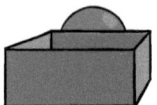

behind

後ろ

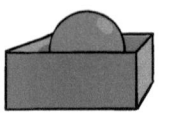

in

中

in front of

前

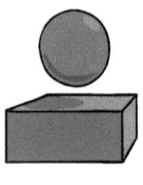

over

上

on

上

under

下

beside

横

between

間

place

場所